COMBATTING SHAMING
and Toxic Communities™

# COMBATTING
# BODY
# SHAMING

TAMRA B. ORR

ROSEN
PUBLISHING®

New York

Published in 2017 by The Rosen Publishing Group, Inc.
29 East 21st Street, New York, NY 10010

Copyright © 2017 by The Rosen Publishing Group, Inc.

First Edition

**Library of Congress Cataloging-in-Publication Data**

Names: Orr, Tamra, author.
Title: Combatting body shaming / Tamra B. Orr.
Description: First Edition. | New York : Rosen Publishing, 2017. | Series:
  Combatting shaming and toxic communities | Audience: Grades 7-12. |
  Includes bibliographical references and index.
Identifiers: LCCN 2015049668 | ISBN 9781508171140 (library bound)
Subjects: LCSH: Body image in children--Juvenile literature. | Body
  image--Juvenile literature. | Child psychology--Juvenile literature.
Classification: LCC BF723.B6 O77 2016 | DDC 306.4/613--dc23
LC record available at http://lccn.loc.gov/2015049668

*Manufactured in China*

# CONTENTS

# INTRODUCTION

When it comes to being offensive, Canadian comedian Nicole Arbour is a star. With thousands of followers on her YouTube channel and Facebook page, she knows people are listening to her. She has produced videos on such controversial topics as race, religion, and even refugees. The former cheerleader does it all with a blonde "airhead" attitude and a perky smile. Most of the time, despite the topics, people seem to find her pretty funny.

All of that changed in September 2015 when Arbour's new video "Dear Fat People" was posted on YouTube. For six minutes, the comedian made fun of the idea of "fat shaming," saying it was something overweight people made up to get sympathy. "I don't feel bad for you because you are taking your body for granted," she stated in her video. "What are you going to do, fat people? What are you going to do? You going to chase me? I can get away from you by walking at a reasonable pace."

If Arbour was looking for a response to her latest video, she got it. Quickly, it gained more than twenty-five million views. While she did get some chuckles and support for her diatribe against overweight people, she mostly got a negative backlash.

A number of celebrities spoke out against Arbour's negative and offensive message. Whitney Way Thore, star of TLC's *My Big Fat Fabulous Life* posted a video response to YouTube that quickly racked up millions of views. "Fat-shaming is a thing; it's a

Bodies come in all shapes, sizes, and colors. Learning to accept all of the differences among us is the first step in putting an end to the destructive practice of body shaming.

really big thing, no pun intended," she stated. "It is the really nasty spawn of a larger parent problem called body-shaming, which I'm fairly certain everyone on the planet, especially women, has experienced. The next time you see a fat person, you don't know whether that person has a medical condition that caused them to gain weight," she continued. "You don't know if their mother just died. You don't know if they're depressed or suicidal or if they just lost 100 pounds. You don't know."

Arbour is not sorry for what she said because she said it in the hopes that it might inspire people to exercise and follow a healthier diet. She also meant her video to just . . . be funny. "I feel it's really important that we make fun of everybody," she said in an interview. "I think [what] brings us together and unites us as people is that we can poke fun at all of us." On the talk show *The View*, Arbour added, "I'm just being silly. I'm just having a bit of fun and that's what we did! . . . We all need to relax, laugh at everyone, and learn to turn off something we don't like."

Why did Arbour's video about fat shaming seem to hit such a nerve? Chances are because it touched more people than she could have imagined. Fat shaming, as Thore stated, is just one aspect of a bigger cultural problem: body shaming. In modern American society, the window of acceptable body types seems impossibly narrow. If a person is overly thin or rather fat, incredibly tall or quite short, ridicule and embarrassment are almost sure to follow. In the United States, thanks to fashion magazines and other advertisements, it is clear that to be truly attractive, you have to be tall (but not too tall) and thin (but not too thin). If you don't fit those parameters, you are at risk of being called names, having your intelligence and work ethic questioned, and, in general, being shamed for the body that you have. Shame on you for eating too much—or not enough. Why couldn't you grow five more—or fewer—inches?

Body shaming is lethal to a person's self-esteem. If a person's self-esteem is damaged, everything from depression, anxiety, and eating disorders can follow. It is time for it to end, and for people to realize that trying to fit into that tiny window of our culture's standards is not only impossible; it's ridiculous.

# FOR SHAME!

**W**hat do you see when you look in the mirror? Do you see an attractive person? Do you smile at your image? If you do, that is wonderful. If you don't, however, you are not alone. Even if you aren't smiling, many businesses across the world are. After all, if you liked your body shape, your facial features, your hair color and style, and your over-all appearance, why in the world would you try to change

Often what we see in the mirror is not what the rest of the world sees. We tend to be the greatest critics of our own appearance.

any of it? And if you aren't in the market to change anything, you are a lousy consumer.

A number of businesses thrive on the fact that most people look in the mirror and see something that upsets or disappoints them. They think they would look better with more or less hair, if they gained or lost weight, or if they had less acne or bigger muscles. But don't worry, the media reassures people: We have just the product you need for that.

# PRESSURE AT HOME

The pressure to lose weight and to be thin sometimes comes from the people who care about you the most: your parents. The day they became mom and dad, they were put in charge of making sure you were fed when you were hungry. As you grew, however, that responsibility became yours. What happens when a parent thinks the choices being made are the wrong ones? What happens when a drive to help you make healthy choices becomes an unhealthy pressure to diet?

For Sandra, much of the pressure to lose weight came from home. "I was constantly told I was fat as a kid," she recalls. "My mother put me on *horrific* diets ... drinking cider vinegar and honey before meals, eating nothing but boiled chicken breasts, living on 800 calories a day. I was a comfortable size sixteen, but that was both ugly and fat to my mom. She had all sorts of torture exercise machines that I had to use. My self-concept was in the minus numbers," Sandra adds. "Gym classes were a nightmare because by high school, I was convinced I was the ugliest, fattest, most inadequate person in class. I think my mother was unhappy with her own body and wanted me to be perfect—in her eyes," continues Sandra. As a child, Sandra attempted to run away many times. "Loaded my toys and books in my wagon, and headed into the woods," she says. "I never succeeded, but I did try."

Today Sandra is quite thin but struggles with an eating disorder that makes it almost impossible for her to eat whenever she is under any kind of stress. She has two grown daughters, whom she has made a point of never controlling through dieting or shaming. When her mother ordered weight loss videos for Sandra's daughters, she "pitched a fit" and would not allow her girls to see them.

Sandra's advice for young people who may be experiencing this type of fat shaming, especially from parents, is to find something that "makes you feel beautiful inside since that is where beauty comes from. Be it art, music, or literature—find anything you love."

Every day people are exposed to hundreds and hundreds of messages about what it means to be attractive. There are magazine and newspaper ads, television commercials, billboards, and display windows. Each one portrays images of the "perfect" people—the thin, chic, stylish, young people who represent the ideal look. As Aimee Nicole Hoffmann writes in *The Beauty Ideal: Unveiling Harmful Effects of Media Exposure to Children,*

> Driving the public's conception of beauty by sending powerful messages about physical perfection everywhere we turn, the media is considered the most influential education medium in existence today. It is manipulative and misleading in nature, and it continues to perpetuate harmful implications about ideal beauty despite solid evidence of damaging effects to people of all ages. To maximize profits, the multi-billion dollar media industry deliberately targets messages of physical perfection to children and young adults during the most impressionable stages of their lives.

Insecurity about your appearance is bad enough, but what happens when the people around you begin to comment on your looks? What happens when there are whispers as you walk by or snide comments mumbled just loud enough for you to hear? What happens when a stranger walks by you and calls you a name based on your looks? All of these are examples of body shaming, and they are painful to experience. Worst of all, they can damage a person's self-esteem so badly that they become depressed and fall prey to eating disorders like anorexia or bulimia.

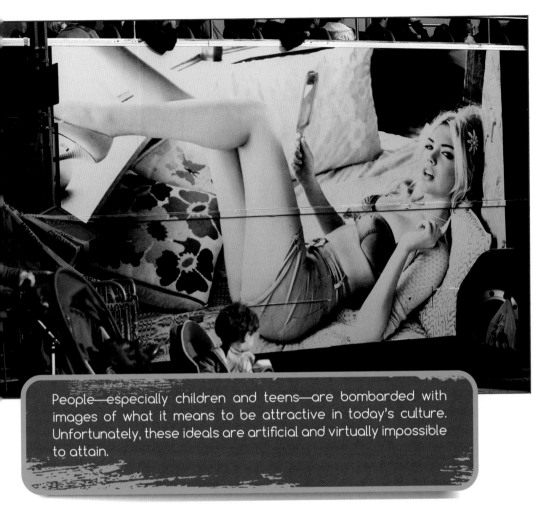

People—especially children and teens—are bombarded with images of what it means to be attractive in today's culture. Unfortunately, these ideals are artificial and virtually impossible to attain.

Claire Mysko, CEO of National Eating Disorders Association (NEDA), has been working in the field of eating disorders and body education for twenty years. She is the author of *You're Amazing! A No-Pressure Guide to Being Your Best Self.* "Our tabloid culture has taken body shaming to new heights, making the language of body shaming commonplace everywhere we turn—from magazine headlines in the grocery checkout to comments in our social media feeds," she stated in an interview with the author. "Traditionally, advertisers and marketers have taken the approach that when we feel bad about ourselves, we are more likely to spend money on products that promise to make us more 'perfect.'"

Body shaming can come in many different forms, from different people. People who are too anything are often the targets. Whether you are exceptionally tall or short or very thin or overweight, you may have been called hurtful nicknames or have known that people were talking about you. They might have said something directly to you or indirectly to another person.

# THE WRONG BODY TYPE

It is hard to imagine when watching Misty Copeland, the first African American female soloist the American Ballet Theatre has had in over twenty years, that this strong woman was ever rejected for her body. Fortunately, she did not listen to what she was told. Instead she has become a true dancing sensation.

Copeland did not begin dancing until she was thirteen—a decade later than most professional dancers get their starts. She learned her first steps at a

Boys and Girls Club in California on a basketball court in her socks.

It did not take long before she was told she absolutely had the "wrong body type" to be a ballet dancer. She did not have a long enough torso, and she was too short. When she transformed into her adult body, the criticism grew. She developed curves, including a bust, hips, and backside. The message was, "you're not what ballet looks like," which she revealed in an interview on the *Today* show. Copeland began binge eating. "I realized that bingeing wasn't a logical reaction," she wrote in an article for *Self* magazine, "but at night, when I was alone, I got so angry: *Who do they think they're talking to? I have so much talent. I'll eat what I want.*"

Finally, Copeland accepted that her body's changes were natural and valid. "So my priority became simply accept my new self," she writes. "I focused on what I wanted to feel good, to be confident in my skin again, to dance." Copeland did not make herself stop bingeing, but instead changed her attitudes about what she ate. "I started thinking about food not as solace but as the fuel that gave me energy and strength I needed to dance—and to live," she admits.

Over the year, she dropped a few pounds but grew proud of her curves. "My body was still different than it had been," she continues. "But now I owned it. My curves began to be an integral part of who I am as a dancer, not something I needed to lose to become one. . . and I think I changed everyone's mind about what a perfect dancer is supposed to look like."

In many instances, body shaming is actually a type of bullying, and it is done as a way of making people feel better about themselves by making fun of someone else. Other times, body shaming is subtle—and can even happen when a person is not aware of it. Are you a body shamer? Before you say yes or no, ask yourself these questions:

- Do you find yourself feeling superior to someone who is overweight or underweight?
- Do you make jokes about people's bodies in public?

At Lincoln Center in autumn 2015, Misty Copeland proved once again that body shape is not the key factor in becoming a world class dancer. Fortunately, Copeland did not listen to those who tried to discourage her.

- Do you tease people about their bodies in an attempt to be "funny"?
- Do you laugh when your friends or family make fun of people because they are overweight or underweight, because they have large or small breasts, or for some other body-related reason?
- Do you always assume that someone's weight is a result of lifestyle choice?
- Do you make assumptions about people's intelligence and personal character based on weight or body shape?

"Body shaming is toxic," Mysko stresses. "It's easy to get caught up in thinking that it's acceptable or the norm, because it's all around us in the media we consume. But it can do real and lasting damage," she adds. Research has shown that people who have been regularly body shamed often deal with a higher rate of suicidal thoughts.

Making fun of people because of their appearance is unkind—and it is incredibly unhelpful. A number of studies have shown that shaming people for their weight does not inspire or motivate them to lose or gain weight. Instead, it just makes them feel worse about themselves and become more stressed. That, in turn, means that if they are barely eating any food, they may stop entirely. If they are already overeating, they may eat even more.

Body shaming hurts. It is dangerous—and it is never the right answer.

# THE FEAR OF FAT

**C**an you guess what 80 percent of ten-year-old girls are most afraid of?

Their parents getting divorced? No.

Getting seriously ill? No.

Flunking a grade? No.

More than 80 percent of these young girls are afraid . . . of getting fat.

In the United States, the number one type of body shaming is targeted at people who are overweight. Every ad for everything from the newest sports car to the latest fashion trend uses long, tall, slim women to sell products. Thin is in. Fat is just . . . more than out.

Because of this cultural perception, overweight people are shamed in any number of ways. Studies have shown that not only do many people see obese people as unattractive, but also lower class and less intelligent. According to the Obesity Organization, "In an extreme form, [weight] stigma can result in both subtle and overt forms of discrimination, such as employment discrimination where an obese employee is denied a position or promotion due to his or her appearance, despite being appropriately qualified."

Overweight people often struggle to be accepted as they are. They are often automatically condemned for not caring about their health or nutrition. The overwhelming perception is that they have no respect for themselves.

Other studies have shown that fat people are often perceived as lazy, sloppy, and lacking in willpower or self-discipline.

Body shaming is more than direct looks or comments. It can also be indirect. Overweight people struggle with daily issues such as fitting into chairs and seats or finding comfortable clothing.

# BANNING THE F WORD

Florida's Obesity Action Coalition (www.obesityaction. org) is a national group that dedicates its efforts to standing up for anyone who has been victimized by fat shaming. One of their most important projects is the petition to "Ban the F Word." According to their website,

> One word doesn't define you.
> One word isn't who you are.
> One word isn't what you see.
> You're more than one word.

"Fat-shaming doesn't discriminate based on race, gender, or socioeconomic status," said Joe Nadglowski, president and CEO of OAC. "The fact that today we use it as an adjective and shame people dealing with the disease of obesity is highly unacceptable. As chair of the weight bias committee, I know individuals, especially children, are often targeted and shamed for their weight. 'Ban the F Word' will raise awareness of this alarming trend and hopefully put a stop to its pervasiveness." The OAC invites people to go to their online petition and sign it. In part, the petition states,

"Fat-shaming is never right, never funny and never acceptable. I am committed to stand-up to fat-shaming wherever I see it, and to 'Ban the F Word' from being used with the intent of hurting or belittling. . . . I will fight with OAC for a world free of weight bias, and will raise awareness that fat-shaming must end. I respectfully ask the media, members of the entertainment industry, healthcare professionals, employers, educators, and all members of the general public to commit to no longer shaming any individual for their weight . . ."

Lori recalls the direct and indirect issues she has had to deal with. "In elementary school, I got called the usual names: hippo, elephant, wide load, etc. In gym class, I got routinely picked last for teams," she recalls in an interview with the author. "Now, as an adult, I've been asked if I was pregnant or when my baby was due. Clothing my size is only available in special stores. Conference rooms almost always have chairs with arms into which I won't fit. Cars are no longer available with the bench seats I find most comfortable. I'd like to buy a new car right now but can't find a single one with a driver's seat into which I fit."

Coping with rude comments has been challenging. "I've used humor as a defense mechanism," she explains. "You can't laugh at me if I'm either laughing with you or I beat you to making a joke in the first place." Lori has also learned, with age, to stand up for herself when she needs to. "I no longer squeeze into chairs that are painfully tight," she says. "I ask someone to bring me another chair or I go find one for myself." Today,

One problem many overweight people deal with is trying to find places to sit comfortably. This is especially true on airplanes, where seats are very small and pushed together tightly.

Lori's goals are to be healthy and happy. She advises all young people to remember to stand up for their rights. "Humans, no matter their size, all have the same rights," she says. "I wish I had realized sooner that my body is what it is, and even if my goal is to be smaller someday, I have the right to respect and equitable treatment now."

## Medical Shaming

Angela found herself being fat shamed at her doctor's office. After seeing a new doctor for her chronic knee problems, she was dismissed with a cursory, "If you lost some weight, maybe that wouldn't be a problem." She was shocked. Her knee problem began when she was much thinner—and the inability to walk without pain was what had caused the weight gain in the first place. It was a bitter lesson for Angela. "I didn't know if I

In a number of instances, medical professionals end up body shaming their patients. When every health problem is attributed to the need to lose weight, it is easy for patients to feel overlooked and dismissed.

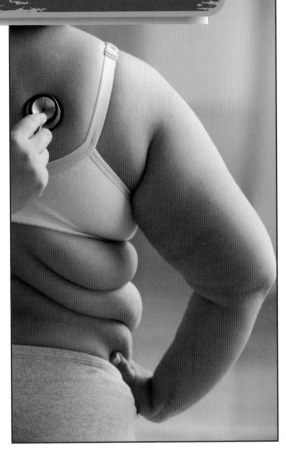

could say anything about the shaming without irreparably damaging the relationship I was trying to build with the doctor." She is slowly learning to stand up for herself, however. "I am a responsible, educated, powerful person who also happens to be fat," she says. "All of the things I am don't matter to some people in whose eyes I am nothing more than my weight but . . . I AM more than my weight."

Lea was tired of being in pain. Her side hurt daily; sometimes, the pain was unbearable. She suspected she had kidney stones so went to her provider to ask his thoughts. He playfully punched her in the side and said, "You didn't scream, so no, you don't have kidney stones. You just need to lose weight and you'll feel better." Lea went home discouraged and depressed. Three months later, she had emergency surgery to remove kidney stones. "Doctors tend to take one look at me and decide every single complaint I have comes from being overweight," she says.

Lea is not alone in her experience. Research has shown that more than half of doctors describe their overweight patients as "ugly, awkward, and non-compliant." Many patients who are overweight report feeling less respected by their physicians, and a number refuse to seek medical care because they don't want to feel ridiculed or embarrassed by their doctors.

Every year, the Binge Eating Disorder Association sponsors the Weight Stigma Awareness Week. Held over five days, each day a different theme is discussed and a wide variety of people share their stories and experiences. In 2015, one topic was Weight Stigma in the Provider Community. This lecture focused on the number of physicians who commonly blame every patient complaint or symptom from an overweight patient on weight. As presenter and dietician Blair Mize, MS, RND, LDN, CLC stated, "Too often, larger people are criticized, shamed, and misunderstood because of their weight. Furthermore, the perception of many healthcare providers remains that 'if people would just lose weight, they could be healthy.'" She adds, "It's time all health professionals learn that the number on the scale does not define a person's health, worth, or value. Our patients are human beings, not human bodies, and they deserve evidence-based guidance, rather than judgment, shame or 'easy answers.'"

# In the Spotlight

If anyone understands the power and pain of body shaming, it is celebrities. Since they are always in the public eye—and the focus of countless photographs—gaining even a few extra

Despite a successful career, Gabourey Sidibe is often targeted by body shaming trolls for her size. The Academy Award-nominated actress has been applauded for speaking out against fat shamers.

pounds can start the criticism. In recent years, a number of famous people have spoken out against the trend of body shaming. Famous retorts have come from Selena Gomez, Tyra Banks, Kelly Clarkson, and Jennifer Lawrence. After reading some comments made about her weight, actor Emma Stone told *USA Today*, "I firmly believe that nothing really affects you or can really bother you if you don't already feel that way about yourself. . . . We're always too skinny or too fat or too tall or too short. . . We're shaming each other and we're shaming ourselves, and it sucks." Actor Gabourey Sidibe has been body shamed countless times. Finally she tweeted, "To people making mean comments about my Golden Globes pics, I mos def cried about it on that private jet on my way to my dream job last night."

Making decisions about a person's personality, intelligence, and character based on weight is as ridiculous and unjustified as making that decision based on a person's height, skin color, or religion. Body shaming overweight people is a form of bullying, and it does not help anyone.

# OTHER TYPES OF
# BODY SHAMING

**W**hen Sheri was in elementary school, she hated gym class. She tried to hide and change her clothes where no one could see her. She did not want to hear the questions she would inevitably be asked.

"Don't you ever eat?"

"Doesn't your mom feed you?"

"Why are you so boney?"

Instead of being shamed for being overweight, Sheri was ridiculed for being overly thin. "I used to wear long underwear under my pants to try and look bigger," she admits. Feeling defensive, Sheri would often yell that yes, of course, she ate. She just didn't gain any weight. "Kids were cruel," she recalls. "I wish I had been more outspoken and defended myself more." Sheri tried to gain weight for years but was not able to until age thirty-five. "It is surprising how strangers, family, and just people in general will so boldly make comments to you about your weight," she adds.

Fat shaming is not the only type of body shaming. Some people engage in making women feel inadequate for being underweight and not having a "feminine" shape. This leads many to wonder what is an acceptable body type.

## When Thin Is Too Thin

Body shaming is certainly not limited to people who are over-weight. Our culture's narrow window of body acceptance excludes many different types of people: fat, skinny, short, tall—even pregnant.

Skinny or thin shaming, as it is called, is making fun of people who are underweight. The types of comments these people often hear include, "You look anorexic!" "You're a toothpick," "You should put some meat on those bones," "Real women have curves, you know," "You look like a stick figure," and "You look like a boy."

"My family members were always calling me 'string bean' and 'bean pole,'" says Donna. She was called names at home and school and was finally taken to the doctor to make sure she was all right. "I just became introverted and hid my feelings," she adds. She felt like she had to be doing something wrong. "I used to ask why there are so many diet books to lose weight, but nothing for people to gain weight," she explains. "I thought I must be a freak of nature."

As an adult, she still cannot gain weight. "I still hear, 'You need to put some meat on your bones, so eat!'" she says. "I eat—I eat quite a bit, but I just cannot gain weight."

Just as making assumptions about overweight people is damaging, so is making assumptions about those on the opposite end of the spectrum. There is no doubt that American culture respects and values thin over fat, but there is a limit to just how thin is considered acceptable. Fifty years ago, "fat" was a size eighteen and up, while today anyone who wears a size eight or above is considered "plus size." The window of what is acceptable is constantly changing and what is appealing and ideal today most likely will not be tomorrow.

## Too Tall or Too Short

Although height is something that is mostly genetically determined, someone who is too short or too tall often faces body-shaming comments as well. Girls who are "too tall" and men who are "too short" are especially teased. Many of them find it more difficult than most to find people to date because their height—or lack of it—is not fitting into the cultural ideal.

# AROUND THE WORLD

Body shaming is not unique to the United States. It happens all around the world. In the states, according to a 2011 survey conducted by *Glamour* magazine, the number of U.S. women who have had an "I hate my body" moment is an astounding ninety-seven percent. But Americans are not alone: Eating disorders are spreading across the globe as people attempt to get that "perfect body."

People are fighting against body shaming, however—sometimes in very unusual ways. For example, in March 2015, a photo of an overweight man dancing in London went viral. The person who posted the original picture captioned it with, "Spotted this specimen trying to dance the other week. He stopped when he saw us laughing." Cassandra Fairbanks, an L.A.-based journalist, spotted this post and began searching for the dancing man. In less than twenty-four hours, the man, Sean O'Brien, had been located. Fairbanks issued an invitation to O'Brien, which read:

Dancing Man,
We don't know much about you, but a photo on the internet suggested that you wanted to dance and were made to feel like you shouldn't be.

We want to see you dance freely and if you would have us, we would love to dance with you.

We are prepared to throw quite the dance party just for you, if you'd have us.

To be clear, it's 1,727 of us. And we are all women. If this isn't appealing, we're ok with taking no for an answer, but we'd like you to know—the offer stands.

May we have this dance?

—An occasionally overly enthusiastic group of young women in California

In addition to being a lot of fun, this unique dance party raised $70,000 for antibullying charities and positive body-image programs throughout the United States and United Kingdom.

Cynthia is not a particularly tall woman, but she grew early, hitting five feet five inches (165 centimeters) when she was still in elementary school. "We were always lined up short to tall, so I was always the second from the back. I equated shortness with being petite and feminine," she adds in an interview with the author. She remembers her thin mother being shamed, too. "She was told she had a figure like 'an ironing board tied around the middle'," Cynthia recalls. "She never believed she was beautiful, not even in her 20's when people thought she was a model."

Cynthia did not respond to the teasing she got but instead "took it in without comment." However, she is sure those days of being teased for her height played a role in her eating disorders.

Short boys and tall girls are fairly common in elementary school, thanks to the difference in the gender's growth spurts. If those height differences continue into adulthood, however, it can be challenging for everyone.

"My goal was not only to be ultimately thin, but just SMALLER— more feminine in my mind," she recalls. "I advise people to ask themselves what they value in a person, and what qualities are important in a friend," suggests Cynthia. "That can be a real wake up call. Appearance is meaningless, despite what the media tries to tell us."

Men who are shorter than the average also deal with their own type of body shaming. Some of the comments made by these men include, "I feel like, as a short guy, any attempt to look cool just ends up looking silly," "I'm a short male and I try my best to accept and love myself, but I hate it," and "I'm a short guy and find it hard to get girls to like me. Being called 'cute' isn't a compliment." Shorter men say they find it harder to be taken seriously, and some rely on a sense of humor to cover up a lack of confidence.

## Pregnancy Shaming

Being pregnant means many things, from shifting hormones to changing body shape. One thing that it should not include is any kind of body shaming. Yet, in our culture, it often does.

Gain "too much weight," a judgment that varies greatly according to care provider, body size, and point in pregnancy, and you will likely be criticized. If you happen to be a celebrity, you are sure to see that negativity reflected in the headlines. Pregnant Kim Kardashian was compared to a killer whale. Hayden Panettiere was shown with the words "huge" and "GIANT" under her pregnant photos. However, as one reporter

Celebrities are often chased by photographers even when fully pregnant. It is common for pregnant women to be negatively labeled and shamed, as beauty icon Kim Kardashian learned.

said online, "growing the gift of life is no time to have to deal with haters."

Katie Fehlinger, a meteorologist for CBS3 in Philadelphia, Pennsylvania, was body shamed when she was pregnant with twins in summer 2015. Some viewers complained about how she dressed. Others thought she should not be on camera since she was so pregnant. Some viewers even wrote in, calling the mother-to-be such names as "sausage in a casing" and "blimp." It was hurtful to her, and on Fehlinger's Facebook page she wrote, "Frankly, I don't care how 'terrible' or 'inappropriate' anyone thinks I look. I will gladly gain 50 pounds and suffer sleepless, uncomfortable nights if it means upping my chances to deliver 2 healthy baby girls."

Despite the comments, Fehlinger stayed on the air until shortly before she had her twins on August 26. Now that her pregnancy is over, it is time for viewers to keep a close eye on how fast she loses her pregnancy weight, of course. As the reporter for Philly. com wrote, "Fehlinger will be under a lot of scrutiny, especially in this age of celebrity post-baby body-flaunting. But Heidi Klum, who returned to a Victoria's Secret runway six weeks after giving birth to her fourth child, is a freak of nature. You can't put those kinds of expectations on real-life working moms. It's just not fair. But people do all the time—which is what led to Fehlinger being pregnancy-shamed when all she wanted was to do her job."

# FOUR

# TO REACT—OR RESPOND?

**T**here is no question about it: being body shamed for anything about your appearance is painful. It hurts feelings, damages self-esteem, and might tempt you to engage in unhealthy or even dangerous behavior. Body shaming is a type of bullying and it is something that you need to respond to before a few people's unkind comments and behavior ruin what you see when you look in the mirror.

When people make judgments about a person's weight, it can dramatically affect what and how a person eats—or doesn't eat.

Dr. Serena Wadhwa, author, coach, counselor, and clinical psychologist, works with a number of people who struggle with body image issues, often due to some type of body shaming. "Shaming tends to be something that has had a presence throughout much of time," she says in an interview with the author. "Most individuals base what they 'should' look like by other people's standards, rather than on what is healthy and effective for themselves." As a counselor, Wadhwa sees the damage that shaming can do and how it can lead to bigger problems. "Individuals may develop other issues resulting from the shame and insecurities," she explains. "They may engage in substance abuse to manage some of the emotions. Eating disorders and other struggles may result as well. These become vicious cycles that may reinforce shaming thoughts, behaviors, and actions."

# AN INSTAGRAM STAR

When Australian teenager Essena O'Neill began posting to Instagram and YouTube, it did not take long for her to get thousands of followers and subscribers. O'Neill embodies the physical appearance that is considered almost perfect in American culture: tall, slim, blonde hair, blue eyes. It was not long before she was getting offers to be a professional model.

Behind all of the social media posts, however, was an unhappy young woman. "I fell in love with this idea I could be of value to other people," O'Neill admitted in an online article. "Let's call this my snowballing addiction to be liked by others. . . I was severely addicted. I believed how many likes and followers I had correlated to how many people liked me. . . social media had become my sole identity. I didn't even know what I was without it."

To achieve the "perfect look" O'Neill was restricting calories and exercising excessively. Her bikini shots, which were made to look perfectly natural, were actually perfectly staged—and sponsored by a particular brand. "I just want younger girls to know this isn't candid life, or cool or inspirational," she wrote. "It's contrived perfection made to get attention." She says to capture that one casual-looking selfie she posted online, she spent hours putting on makeup, curling her hair, changing outfits, and then taking more than fifty shots before choosing one. Before posting it, she would edit it with a variety of apps to make sure she looked her best.

Since then, O'Neill has focused on posting shots of herself without any makeup. She has also taken to the web to encourage young people to take a break from social media in order to move away from social approval. "Each one of us is powerful enough to create great changes," she writes. "Let us just begin with one."

# Making a Choice

Before you start making some choices about how to handle being body shamed or seeing your friends and others doing it to someone else, take a moment to ask yourself if you know the difference between *reacting* to a situation and *responding* to one.

When you accidentally reach out and touch something hot with your fingers, you react. You jerk your hand away as fast as possible. Your reaction is quick, thoughtless, and usually involves emotions of panic and feelings of pain. Reactions are typically defensive. On the other hand, when you are asked a question, you respond. A

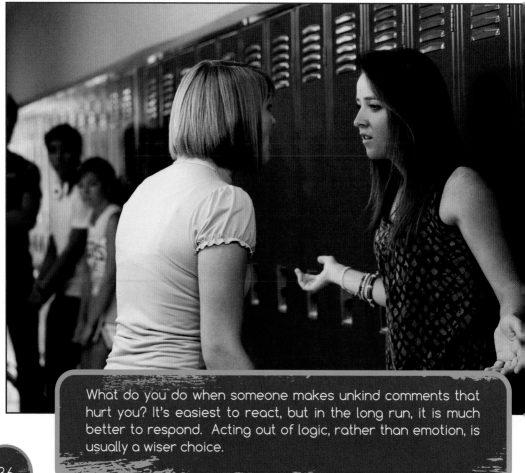

What do you do when someone makes unkind comments that hurt you? It's easiest to react, but in the long run, it is much better to respond. Acting out of logic, rather than emotion, is usually a wiser choice.

response is usually a considered, thoughtful, reasoned action as opposed to a knee-jerk reaction.

If you are teased about your body in some way, whether it be in person or on any of the modes of social media available today (Facebook, Twitter, Tumblr, Instagram, Snapchat, etc.), it is easy to lash out and react to the hurt. As with your burned finger, you want the pain to stop, so you move rapidly. You let emotion guide your words or actions, and you may end up doing or saying something that you will regret. Instead of reacting, it is more effective if you can respond.

This may sound like wise advice, but how can you respond to unkind comments, looks, or attitudes? Here are some possible responses:

"Why are we focusing on flaws? Let's focus on what we love about ourselves!"

"That is a hurtful thing to say. Please stop."

"I feel beautiful/handsome/attractive just as I am, thank you!"

Of course, ignoring the comments is another viable response. Sometimes turning your back and realizing someone's opinion is not worth responding to at all can be the best choice of all.

Celebrities are used to being body shamed. They often respond in very positive ways. Selena Gomez responded to negative posts by stating on Instagram, "I love being happy with me y'all #theresmoretolove." Kelly Clarkson responded to a nasty tweet by saying, "Oh, she's tweeted something nasty about me? That's because she doesn't know me. I'm awesome! It doesn't bother me. It's a free world. Say what you will." Jennifer Aniston stated, "You're damned if you're too thin and you're damned if you're too heavy. According to the press, I've been both. It's impossible to satisfy everyone and I suggest we stop trying."

# CARDS ON THE SUBWAY

It was a quiet way to express an opinion—and to crush someone's day, all at the same time. In November 2015, a few people riding the London Underground (subway) began handing out cards from a group known as Overweight Haters Ltd. In part, the card read, "Our organization hates and resents fat people. We object to the enormous amount of food resources you consume while half the world starves. . . And we do not understand why you fail to grasp that by eating less you will be better off, slimmer, happy and find a partner."

Bethany Rutter, a journalist and blogger, was appalled when she heard about this and wanted to do something to counteract the cruelty, so she printed out a set of cards that simply said, "You look great today!" She planned to hand them out on the Tube. "I heard about this horrendous fat-phobic campaign of hate on the London underground and thought it was the perfect opportunity to get started on this," stated Rutter to Style.Mic website. A plus-size clothing company called Navabi heard about Rutter's plans and stepped in to help. They sponsored the printing of hundreds of cards (without any branding).

The responses from people who were given one of these positive affirmation cards were wonderful. "Across the board, the reaction was good," says Rutter. "A couple of people asked me what it was about and said they thought it was a good response. Some just took them and said thank you for the compliment."

In a final bit of irony, the Overweight Haters group forgot to register their domain name on the Internet, so Navabi has claimed OverweightHaters.com as their own. Here readers can learn more about their positive cards and download the file to make their own.

Sasha Pieterse, from the popular television show *Pretty Little Liars* had a great response to viewers' comments about her changing weight. She posted a picture of herself on Instagram with the caption, "I am currently under construction . . . thank you for your patience." She also added some advice for young people struggling with weight issues. "I urge and encourage you to please deal with it in a healthy manor [sic]. You and your health are what matters, not anyone else's opinions and assumptions of you. Getting healthy isn't just about working out and eating right . . . it's also about surrounding yourself with those who care about you and want to see you succeed and become the best you can be."

## Self-Talk

Sadly, there are times when the harshest criticism you get regarding your body image comes from yourself. Many people carry around negative self-esteem like a huge, invisible burden that they cannot find a way to put down. It changes what you see in the mirror, how you think about yourself, and how you might respond to anyone body shaming you. Thinking positively about yourself is the number one way to combat the impact of any form of body shaming.

Thinking positively about how you look can be challenging. After all, both our culture and media work hard to make sure you do just the opposite. Your insecurities mean sales and profits for countless businesses. One way to create a better relationship with your body and appearance is through the regular use of positive affirmations. The Eating Disorder Hope website recommends that anyone struggling with body image issues use affirmations such as:

- I am beginning to accept myself more and more.
- I am overcoming negativity and building a positive attitude toward myself.
- I am thankful for my body and what it can do for me.
- My body is beautiful and I respect myself.
- I like _____ about myself (insert a compliment for yourself).

Saying statements like these to yourself when you look in the mirror may feel awkward at first but will come to feel normal with practice. With one statement at a time, you can change the way you see yourself—for the positive.

Responding to body shaming is certainly more effective than reacting. A well-thought-out response, even if it does not stop the unpleasant behavior, presents a strong image and establishes a better reputation for your character than lashing out. Responding with insults or getting emotional often gives the person more material to use against you. A calm, positive response, conversely, makes you look like the more mature and compassionate person. Chances are, that will help your self-esteem, too!

# REACHING OUT

**W**hen someone makes an unkind remark about you, either when you are walking down the hall at school, standing in line at the local fast food restaurant, or stopping by one of your favorite social media sites, one thing is clear: it hurts. It can also make you suddenly feel very alone. Feeling lonely might, in turn, feed into your insecurities and result in feelings of sadness and anger.

Dealing with any kind of pain—from physical to emotional—is frequently easier if you have others who understand how you're feeling and what you're going through.

If these emotions keep growing, the risk of suicide or eating disorders becomes very real. Claire Mysko states that, "We know that there is a clear link between weight stigma, bullying, and eating disorders. One study found that 75 percent of individuals struggling with an eating disorder cited bullying as a significant factor in the development of their illness." As the CEO of the National Eating Disorders Association, Mysko has seen many young people who have been shamed because of their body. "This shaming might not be the sole cause of an eating disorder," she explains, "but it can certainly trigger very self-destructive thoughts and behaviors."

Weight stigma is inherently linked to eating disorders, such as bulimia and anorexia. Unfortunately, these conditions will only make life more difficult—and even more dangerous. A nutritionist can help you devise and stick to a healthy eating plan.

# THE ILLUSIONISTS

Sponsored by the Center for Eating Disorders at Sheppard Pratt, a new, fifty-one-minute documentary called *The Illusionists* (http://theillustionists.org) has been released by the Media Education Foundation to schools, libraries, and organizations. It focuses on how the media capitalizes on people's insecurity, recognizing that the happy, satisfied human being makes a terrible consumer. People who like the way they look are far less likely to spend their money on ways to look better—from cosmetic surgeries or fad diet trends to the latest, greatest type of makeup on the market.

As the website for the documentary states, "From New York to Tokyo, relentless propaganda reminds us that we have only one body—and that we have to enhance it. Through advertising and mass media, multibillion-dollar industries (most notably cosmetics, fashion, dieting, and cosmetic surgery) saturate our lives with images of idealized, unattainable beauty, of an 'Official Body' that does not really exist in nature and that can be obtained only through cosmetic surgery... or digital retouching," the film's synopsis continues. "Flawless beauty is on display everywhere: in street ads,

(continued on the next page)

(continued from previous page)

newspapers, magazines, TV, films ... as well as in video games and pornography. The very quantity of these images makes it impossible for people not to be affected by them. Indeed, the ideal consumer is someone who is anxious, depressed and constantly dissatisfied: academic studies from the most respected institutions show that sad people are bigger spenders."

If you are struggling, reach out. "Ask for help," says Wadhwa. "There's no reason you cannot have a healthy relationship with your body and yourself." She recommends working with a professional to learn the tools and strategies that can help you create this relationship. "Talk to someone about what is going on. It's hard to be vulnerable, yet necessary in order to be open to change and love."

The last thing you are is alone. Millions of other people across the world know just how you feel. A number of them are trying to combat body shaming. In fact, according to many sources, the tide is turning.

## A Positive Direction

Body shaming is becoming so well recognized that businesses and social media sites are responding. In 2004, the Dove Campaign for Real Beauty was initiated to change how society sees attractiveness. Dove has launched commercials with female models of all sizes and shown the truth about how much traditional models are Photoshopped and computer altered to look as they do in advertisements.

In September 2015, plus-size women's clothing company Lane Bryant launched a new campaign called "Plus Is Equal." Its motto is, "We believe all woman should be seen and celebrated equally."

Fashion companies are including more plus-sized clothing in their lines—and even featuring plus-size models on the runway. Plus-size retailers such as Lane Bryant started online social media campaigns like #ImNoAngel in response to Victoria's Secret's campaigns. The National Organization of Women has started a Love your Body social movement, which states, "Dear Body, You were never a problem. There is nothing wrong with your size, your curves, your scars, your flaws, your stretch marks or you. It's not your job to look like the people in magazines. It's not your job to look 'pretty'. You're good enough already."

## Plus-Size Empowerment

Becky Jarvis had been going to children's consignment sales for years in order to save money and shop locally. In 2011, she discovered, to her surprise, that while there are forty children's consignment events in the Pacific Northwest region (and thousands across the country), there were virtually no plus-size consignment events. She wanted to change that. Five years later, Curvy Chic Closet is the only such event in the Pacific Northwest. It features more than two hundred consigners and more than twenty thousand consigned items. It also features the largest plus-size fashion show on the West Coast.

Curvy Chic Closet has more than clothes for plus-sized people, however. "Sometimes there is a notion that if someone

isn't a size fourteen that they cannot come to the event because they think all we have is just clothing," says Jarvis in an interview with the author. "One of our best-kept secrets is we have a fabulous gently used purse, shoes, and jewelry section. We welcome all to our event, including women that may not be plus size, as well as transgender folk. We also strive to make the event a welcoming place by making sure our event location is ADA accessible."

Actor Melissa McCarthy has often spoken out against fat-shaming. As a well-known plus-size celebrity, she is a reminder that talent and beauty have little to do with size. McCarthy also designs a clothing line that includes plus-sizes

Jarvis was shocked when women came up to her in tears at the sales. "I didn't realize just how much I was inspiring and empowering women," she admits. She encourages young people to love their bodies and ignore the body shaming. "It's okay to be tall, short, thin, fat, curvy, or skinny," she says. "Those words are just descriptors and don't mean you are any less of a person. Don't wait until you are in your middle ages to finally realize you're beautiful."

# Where to Find Help

Whether you are being body shamed or you have found yourself body shaming others, you might recognize that you need help. But where can you turn? Good question. Start by looking to the people you trust the most to help you with any problems you might have: your parents, any siblings, close relatives, teachers, or school counselors. If they don't have the answers, they can usually help connect you to the people and professionals who do.

Here are a few more suggestions:

- Spend some time online checking out the many websites that are designed to help people just like you. It often helps with that feeling of isolation you may deal with daily.
- Check out free resources online such as the National Eating Disorders Association's toll-free helpline (800-931-2237) and its body positive organization Proud2Bme.org.
- Consider consulting a physician to make sure your weight or height issues are not the result of a medical condition.
- See a professional dietician for nutritional advice. Dieticians often know many ways to make it easier to lose or to gain weight and do it in a healthy way.
- Engage in some kind of physical activity you like, as it often

helps with self-esteem, along with weight and overall health. You don't have to start running a mile every day (unless it sounds fun!), but perhaps joining a dance class, a walking club, or a school club that focuses on some type of sport you enjoy.

- Avoid looking at or reading any media that supports the body shaming philosophy. (Hint: this means every magazine on the newsstand next to the grocery store cash register.)
- Get actively involved in antishaming campaigns. Many of them are looking for volunteers.
- Spend time talking with people you feel like shaming. You will learn a lot about looking beyond their appearance.
- Speak up when you see something offensive on any of the social media sites you use. Make it clear that that type of treatment is bullying and should not be tolerated. Consider reporting these kinds of comments to the website's moderator.
- Write a letter to the editor of your local or school newspaper about the issue of body shaming.
- Learn about current legislation about body shaming as a type of bullying. Share what you have found with your school.
- Create a petition to stop body shaming in your school. Coordinate with your teachers on how to promote and educate the student body about the issue.

# Health at Every Size Movement

The Association for Size Diversity and Health (ASDAH) is a national group that works to foster education, research, and services to "enhance health and well-being, and which are free from weight-based assumptions and weight discrimination." The main focus of the group is the program Health at Every Size (HAES). The principles of HAES are:

- accepting and respecting the diversity of body shapes and sizes
- recognizing that health and well-being are multidimensional and that they include physical, social, spiritual, occupational, emotional, and intellectual aspects
- promoting all aspects of health and well-being for people of all sizes
- promoting eating in a manner that balances individual nutritional needs, hunger, satiety, appetite, and pleasure
- promoting individually appropriate, enjoyable, life-enhancing physical activity, rather than exercise that is focused on a goal of weight loss

The HAES philosophy supports all body shapes and sizes, although it often focuses on fat shaming since American culture zeroes in on that type of body shaming above all. They do not look at obesity as a disease that needs to be cured, as some people—including many physicians and health organizations—do. "If we say obesity is a disease then we must say, on some level, body fat is pathological," they state in their FAQ section. The organization adds, "It is acceptable—necessary, in fact—for science to explore the differences between different body types; i.e., how they function differently, what their different needs are. But once value is placed on those differences, it becomes discriminatory, and that is what is unacceptable."

Sometimes it seems like American culture does little more than judge people. It feels like there is a nonstop stream of reasons to discriminate and ridicule others, from their political viewpoints or their religious beliefs to their annual incomes or gender identification. The window seems especially narrow when it comes to physical appearances. Shaming others for not

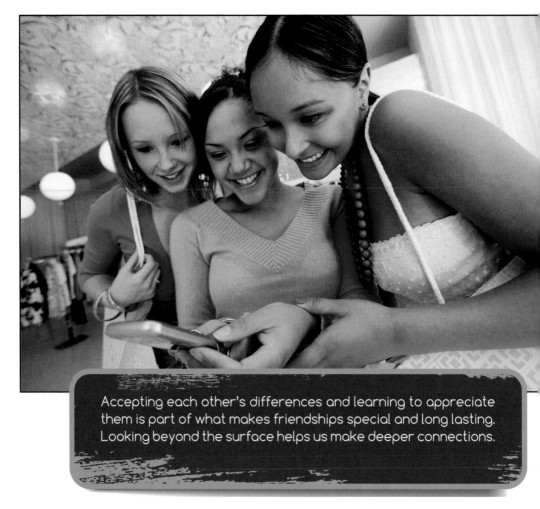

Accepting each other's differences and learning to appreciate them is part of what makes friendships special and long lasting. Looking beyond the surface helps us make deeper connections.

fitting into that very tiny sliver of "body perfection," however, does nothing to improve the world. It does not motivate people to lose or gain weight. In fact, it tends to do just the opposite.

Body shaming helps no one. Instead, the world needs more compassion, kindness, and acceptance. By actively working to combat body shaming, you are making the world a more beautiful place for everyone.

# GLOSSARY

**AFFIRMATION**  A positive statement.

**ANOREXIA**  An eating disorder in which the extreme fear of becoming fat leads one to severely limit food intake.

**BINGE EATING**  Consuming large amounts of food in a short period of time as part of an eating disorder.

**BULIMIA**  An eating disorder in which sufferers binge and purge (vomit) to avoid gaining weight.

**CONTRIVED**  Artificial or unnatural.

**CURSORY**  Brief or superficial.

**DIATRIBE**  A forceful and bitter verbal attack against someone or something.

**EQUITABLE**  Fair or impartial.

**HORRENDOUS**  Extremely unpleasant or terrible.

**INTEGRAL**  Essential or necessary.

**INTROVERTED**  Withdrawn or shy.

**METEOROLOGIST**  A weather forecaster.

**PARAMETERS**  Limitations or boundaries.

**PERPETUATE**  To continue indefinitely.

**PROPAGANDA**  Persuasive publicity.

**SCRUTINY**  Close examination.

**SOCIOECONOMIC**  Having to do with a combination of social and economic factors.

**TORSO**  The chest and abdomen, or trunk, of the human body.

**VIABLE**  Practical or possible.

**VULNERABLE**  Open to physical or emotional attack.

# FOR MORE INFORMATION

Association for Size Diversity and Health (ASDAH)
P.O. Box 3093
Redwood City, CA 94604
877-576-1102
Website: www.sizediversityandhealth.org
The Association for Size Diversity and Health is an international
professional organization whose mission is to "promote
education, research, and the provision of services which
enhance health and well-being, and which are free from
weight-based assumptions and weight discrimination."

Binge Eating Disorder Association (BEDA)
637 Emerson Place
Severna Park, MD 21146
855-855-2332
Website: http://www.bedaonline.com
Since 2008, BEDA has focused on helping those who struggle
with binge eating. Their goal is to "create a community
where people have access to resources to help them
overcome binge eating disorder and its association
conditions in order to live healthy, productive lives free from
weight stigma."

Center for Eating Disorders
111 North First Street Suite 2
Ann Arbor, MI 48104
734-668-85858
Website: http://www.center4ed.org

The Center for Eating Disorders helps connect people with the organizations and professionals they need to answer their questions and get the help they may need.

Families Empowered and Supporting Treatment of Eating Disorders (FEAST)
P.O. Box 11608
Milwaukee, WI 53211
855-50-FEAST
Website: http://www.feast-ed.org
Families Empowered and Supporting Treatment of Eating Disorders focuses on helping parents with support, information, and the wisdom of experience.

National Association of Anorexia Nervosa and Associated Disorders (ANAD)
750 E Diehl Road #127
Naperville, IL 60563
630-577-1333
Website: http://www.anad.org
The National Association of Anorexia Nervosa and Associated Disorders features a helpline, treatment, and links to support groups across the country.

National Association to Advance Fat Acceptance (NAAFA)
P.O. Box 4662
Foster City, CA 94404-0662
916-558-6880
Website: http://www.naafa.org
The National Association to Advance Fat Acceptance is a civil rights organization that helps fight size discrimination. Its

goal is "to help build a society in which people of every size are accepted with dignity and equality in all aspects of life."

National Eating Disorders Association (NEDA)
165 West 46th Street
Suite 402
New York, NY 10036
800-931-2237
Website: www.nationaleatingdisorders.org
National Eating Disorders Association helps anyone dealing
    with anorexia, bulimia, or any other eating disorders.

Obesity Action Coalition (OAC)
4511 N. Himes Avenue Suite 250
Tampa, FL 33614
813-872-7835
Website: http://www.obesityaction.org
Obesity Action Coalition is the group that is working to ban the f
    word and to have fat-shaming apps removed from app
    stores.

Proud2Bme.org
165 West 46th Street
New York, NY 10036
800-931-2237
Website: http://www.proud2bme.org
Proud2Bme is an online community created by and for teens.
    Everything on it is presented with the purpose of promoting
    positive body image and encouraging healthy attitudes
    about weight and food.

United States Association for Body Psychotherapy (USABP)
8639 B 16th Street Suite 119
Silver Spring, MD 20910
Website: http://www.usabp.org
The United States Association for Body Psychotherapy works
   to help people establish good health and to integrate the
   body, mind, and spirit in order to gain well-being.

# Websites

Because of the changing nature of Internet links, Rosen Publishing
has developed an online list of websites related to the subject of
this book. This site is updated regularly. Please use this link to
access the list:

http://www.rosenlinks.com/CSTC/body

# FOR FURTHER READING

Arena, Kasey, and Heather Waxman. *BODYpeace: Release Shame and Discover Body Freedom*. Kingman, AZ: Promoting Natural Health, LLC, 2015

Beck, Debra. *My Feet Aren't Ugly: A Girl's Guide to Loving Herself from the Inside Out*. New York, NY: Beaufort Books, 2011.

Dunham, Kelli. *The Boy's Body Book: Everything You Need to Know for Growing up YOU*. Kennebunkport, ME: Applesauce Press, 2015.

Engdahl, Sylvia. Obesity: Opposing Viewpoints. Farmington Hills, MI: Greenhaven Press, 2014.

Gay, Kathlyn. *Are You Fat? The Obesity Issue for Teens*. Berkeley Heights, NJ: Enslow Publishers, 2014.

Greenhaven Press. *Childhood Obesity*. Farmington Hills, MI: Greenhaven Press, 2016.

Jensen, Diane Mastromarino. *The Girl's Guide to Loving Yourself*. Boulder, CO: Blue Mountain Arts, Inc., 2011.

Kamberg, Mary-Lane. *Women: Body Image and Self-Esteem* (Young Woman's Guide to Contemporary Issues). New York, NY: Rosen Classroom, 2012.

Kilpatrick, Haley, and Whitney Joiner. *The Drama Years: Real Girls Talk about Surviving Middle School—Bullies, Brands, Body Image, and More*. Florence, MA: Free Press, 2012.

Langlois, Carol. *Girl Talk: Boys, Bullies, and Body Image*. Madison, VA: Christine F. Anderson Publishing and Media, 2014.

Libal, Autumn. *Discrimination and Prejudice: Understanding Obesity.* Broomall, PA: Mason Crest Publishers, 2014.

Morrison, Betsy S. Self-Esteem: Teen Mental Health. New York, NY: Rosen Publishing Group, 2011.

Roizen, Michael F. YOU: *The Owner's Manual for Teens: A Guide to a Healthy Body and Happy Life.* New York, NY: Scribner, 2011.

Scherer, Lauri S. *Body Image: Introducing Issues with Opposing Viewpoints.* Farmington Hills, MI: Greenhaven Press, 2012.

Smith, Rita, Vanessa Baish, and Edward Willet. *Self-Image and Eating Disorders (Teen Mental Health).* New York, NY: Rosen Classroom, 2012.

# BIBLIOGRAPHY

Arbour, Nicole. "Dear Fat People." Youtube. September 3,, 2015. Retrieved November, 28, 2015. (https://www.youtube.com/watch?v=CXFgNhyP4-A).

Armstrong, Jenice. "Pregnancy-shamed CBS3 meteorologist to return to work next week." Philly.com, November 12, 2015. Retrieved Dec. 11, 2015 (http://mobile.philly.com).

Bried, Erin. "Stretching Beauty: Ballerina Misty Copeland on Her Body Struggles." Self.com, March 18, 2014. Retrieved Dec. 3, 2015 (http://www.self.com/wellness/health/2014/03/ballerina-misty-copeland-body-struggles/).

Dreisbach, Shaun. "Shocking Body-Image News: 97% of Women Will Be Cruel to Their Bodies Today." Glamour.com, February 3, 2011. Retrieved Jan. 21, 2016. (http://www.glamour.com)

Fischer, Erin Mckelle. "9 Body Positive Social Media Campaigns That Are Changing How We Perceive Beauty Both In and Outside the Fashion World." Bustle.com, April 15, 2015. Retrieved December 4, 2015 (http://www.bustle.com).

Hammesfahr, Lexie. "Pregnancy Shaming Is A Real Thing And It's Not OK" ABC Action News, October 19, 2015. Retrieved December, 7, 2015 (http://www.abcactionnews.com/newsy/pregnancy-shaming-is-a-real-thing-and-its-not-ok).

Hammett, Donna, e-mail interview with the author, November 24, 2015.

Hetter, Katia. "Celebrities Battle It Out Over Fat-Shaming." CNN, September 28, 2015. Retrieved December 2, 2015 (http://www.cnn.com/2015/09/06/entertainment/fat-shaming-nicole-arbour/).

Hoffman, Aimee Nicole. "The Beauty Ideal: Unveiling Harmful Effects of Media Exposure to Children." University of Maine. Retrieved November 28, 2015. (http://www.honors.umaine.edu/files/2009/07/hoffmann-2004.pdf).

Jarvis, Becky, e-mail interview with the author, November 18, 2015.

Karges, Crystal. "Body Image and Self-Talk: Do Affirmations Help?" Eatingdisorderhope.com. Retrieved December 10, 2015 (http://www.eatingdisorderhope.com).

Leach, Angela, e-mail interview with the author, November 16, 2015.

Long, Jamie. "Are You a Fat-Shamer?" Psychology Today. September 25, 2013. Retrieved December 6, 2015 (https://www.psychologytoday.com/blog/finding-cloud9/201309/are-you-fat-shamer).

Lubitz, Rachel. "Fat-Shamers Hand Out Nasty Cards on Subway, So Plus-Size Company Has Awesome Response." Style.mic.com, December 1, 2015. Retrieved December 11, 2015 (http://mic.com).

Mize, Blair. "Practicing Weight Neutrality in a Weight-Biased Healthcare System." Bedaonline.com, September 24, 2015. Retrieved December 10, 2015 (http://bedaonline.com)).

Mysko, Claire, e-mail interview with the author, November 23, 2015.

Quinlan, Erin. "'I was born to do this': How ballet star Misty Copeland fought adversity — and won." Today.com, September 4, 2014. Retrieved November 29, 2015 (http://www.today.com/)

Rasemas, Cynthia, e-mail interview with the author, November 25, 2015.

Regan, Helen. "The Fat-Shamed 'Dancing Man' Who Became an Internet Sensation Attends a Party in His Honor in L.A." Time, May 25, 2015. Retrieved December 10, 2015 (http://time.com).

Riordan, Holly. "Stop Body Shaming! Quotes about Loving Your Size ..." Allwomanstalk.com. Retrieved December 10, 2015 (http://inspiration.allwomenstalk.com/stop-body-shaming-quotes-about-loving-your-size).

Rosen, Christopher. "Comedian Nicole Arbour criticized for fat-shaming after 'Dear Fat People' video." Entertainment Weekly, September 7, 2015. Retrieved December 4, 2015 (http://www.ew.com/article/2015/09/07/nicole-arbour-dear-fat-people-video).

Ross, Ashley. "'Dear Fat People' Comedian Nicole Arbour: 'I'm Not Apologizing for This Video.' Time. September 10, 2015. Retrieved December 1, 2015 (http://time.com/4028119/dear-fat-people-nicole-arbour/).

Ross, Carolyn. "I see fat people." Psychologytoday.com. August 7, 2013. Retrieved December 1, 2015 (https://www.psychologytoday.com/blog/real-healing/201308/i-see-fat-people).

Roy, Sandra, e-mail interview with the author, November 13, 2015.

Smith, Lori, e-mail interview with the author, November 15, 2015.

Vandevere, Sheri, e-mail interview with the author, November, 29, 2015.

Wadhwa, Serena, e-mail interview with the author, November, 30, 2015.

# INDEX

# About the Author

Tamra Orr is a full-time author living in the Pacific Northwest. After receiving her bachelor of science degree in English and secondary education from Ball State University, she began writing full time for students of all ages. She has written more than 450 nonfiction books for children and writes a great deal of educational assessment material for both state and national tests. She has dieted since as early as she can remember and knows how painful body shaming can feel. She practices positive affirmations every day and is slowly becoming the person she has always wanted to be. When she is not writing, Orr is camping with her husband and children, reading a book, or writing letters to friends scattered across the globe.

# Photo Credits

Cover Stuart Monk/Shutterstock.com; p. 5 gpointstudio/Shutterstock.com; p. 7 Loretta Ray/The Image Bank/Getty Images; p. 11 © Dan Callister/Alamy Stock Photo; p. 14 Thos Robinson/Getty Images; p. 17 Digital Vision/Thinkstock; p. 20 Stewart Cohen/Blend Images/Getty Images; p. 21 Jose Luis Pelaez Inc/Blend Images/Getty Images; p. 23 Jaguar PS/Shutterstock.com; p. 26 fstop123/E+/Getty Images; p. 30 Justin Pumfrey/The Image Bank/Getty Images; p. 31 Bauer-Griffin/GC Images/Getty Images; p. 33 Cultura RM/Christoffer Askman/Getty Images; p. 36 Weston Colton/Getty Images; p. 41 Zero Creatives/Cultura/Getty Images; p. 42 Alexander Raths/Shutterstock.com; p. 45 Monica Schipper/Getty Images; p. 46 George Pimentel/WireImage/Getty Images; p. 50 Mike Watson Images/moodboard/Thinkstock; cover and interior pages camouflage pattern Lorelyn Medina/Shutterstock.com; cover and interior pages texture patterns Chantal de Bruijne/Shutterstock.com, foxie/Shutterstock.com.

Designer: Nicole Russo; Editor: Christine Poolos;
Photo Researcher: Carina Finn